Romeo and Juliet

by William Shakespeare

CEFR level A1+

Adapted by Karen Kovacs
for
Read Stories – Learn English

Read Stories – Learn English

Read Stories – Learn English

Romeo and Juliet: CEFR level A1+ (ELT Graded Reader)
Original text by William Shakespeare
Adapted text © Karen Kovacs, 2025
Logo © Karen Kovacs, 2025

No part of this book may be reproduced, scanned or distributed in any printed or electronic form without permission. Please do not participate in or encourage piracy of copyrighted materials in violation of the author's rights. Thank you for respecting the hard work of the author.

CONTENTS

What are graded readers?	Page 8
Meet the author	Page 9
People in the story	Page 11
The story	Page 13
Exercises	Page 65
Words from the story	Page 68

WHAT ARE GRADED READERS?

Graded readers are books in easy English. They are written for learners of English and they have **vocabulary and grammar at your level**.

Each book has some new, more difficult words. There are **definitions** for these words at the back of the book.

WHY READ GRADED READERS?

- Studies show that learners who read in English **improve in all areas much more quickly** than learners who don't read.

- With graded readers, you **don't need a dictionary** so reading is more **relaxing**.

- The stories are all in **modern English**.

- You can learn vocabulary and grammar **in context** (this is the best way, according to teachers).

- Reading a book in English will improve your **comprehension**, your **fluency** and your **confidence**.

- The stories are **exciting** and reading them is **fun**!

Meet
the author

My name is Karen.

- I'm the author of many books for English learners.
- I've been nominated 3 times for a Language Learner Literature Award.
- I have a Degree in English Literature and a Master's in Linguistics.
- I'm an experienced English teacher, in the UK and abroad.
- I speak Hungarian, French and Spanish, so I understand how it feels to learn a new language!

Karen Kovacs

ReadStories-LearnEnglish.com

More stories at the same level

New words

When you see a word in **bold**, go to the back of the book. There you will find a definition of the word.

People in the story

The Capulets

Juliet

Old Capulet – Juliet's father

Lady Capulet – Juliet's mother

Tybalt – Juliet's **cousin**

Nanny – a **servant**; she looks after Juliet

The Montagues

Romeo

Old Montague – Romeo's father

Benvolio – Romeo's cousin

Others

Prince Escalus

Mercutio – Romeo's friend

Lawrence the **priest**

Paris – he wants to **marry** Juliet

Romeo and Juliet

CHAPTER 1

Two Families, One Problem

The Italian city of Verona is very old and very beautiful. The weather is warm and life is good. But there is one problem. Two important families – the Montagues and the Capulets – live in Verona and they **fight** often.

It is a hot day in July. Three young Montague men are walking together. They're talking and laughing. They're having fun. Then they see some young Capulet men.

"Why are you looking at me?" says Tybalt Capulet. He takes out his **sword**. "Do you have a problem with me?"

Benvolio Montague stops and he takes out his sword too.

"Yes, I have a big problem with you! You're a Capulet!" he says. "Our family **hates** your family!"

"We hate your family more!" Tybalt answers.

They move closer, their swords in their hands. Their eyes are angry. Their feet are fast. They are ready.

The other men stand behind them. "Yes! Yes!" they say. They are excited – they enjoy watching street fights.

Tybalt hits Benvolio. Then Benvolio hits Tybalt. Sword hits sword again and again.

The people of Verona hear the noise. Mothers run from their homes and they take their children's hands. "Come home," they say. "The streets aren't safe."

Some older men come outside. "Stop fighting!" they **shout**. But the young men don't stop. The older men start fighting too. Now, twenty or more people are hitting, kicking and shouting.

Then Old Capulet arrives. He's the oldest man in the Capulet family. He takes out his sword.

"Stop it!" says his wife. "You're too old!"

"Look! Old Montague is here too!" he says. "I must fight him!"

Old Montague takes out his sword. He wants to fight too.

But before they can use their swords, the most important man in Verona arrives. His name is Prince Escalus.

"All of you, listen to me!" he says.

The young men don't stop fighting.

The Prince gets angry. "Put down your swords NOW!" he shouts.

The fighting stops.

"Capulets! Montagues!" the Prince says.

"Every day, you bring noise and problems to our streets. The people of Verona are angry, and I am too."

The men don't speak. They listen.

"Your families hate **each other**, we all know that," says the Prince. "But you must stop fighting. Do you understand?"

"Yes, we do," they say.

"Go home," the Prince tells them. "Do not fight again! Next time, I will **execute** you. You will die."

Everyone runs home, but Benvolio stays. He doesn't move.

A minute later, Romeo arrives.

"Hello, **cousin**," he says. "Are you ok? Was there a fight again?"

"Yes, there was. But I'm fine, don't worry," says Benvolio. "And you? Are you alright? You look sad."

"I'm **in love**," answers Romeo.

"And that's bad?"

"Yes. She doesn't love me."

"Oh, I see," says Benvolio. He puts a hand on his cousin's arm. "Love is a beautiful thing but it is often hard. What's her name?"

"She's so beautiful," says Romeo.

"That's not a name!" says Benvolio with a smile.

"Her name is Rosaline." Romeo looks down. "I love her so much – I'm going to die."

"Forget her," says Benvolio.

"I can't," answers Romeo. "She's the most beautiful woman in the world."

Benvolio doesn't speak for a minute. Then he says, "I'm going to a party tonight. Come with me. You'll see – there are lots of other beautiful women. Mercutio is coming too."

Mercutio is Romeo's best friend. He likes dancing, laughing and drinking good wine.

"Where is the party?" asks Romeo.

"It's at the Capulets' house."

"What? We can't go there! They hate us."

"They won't see our faces," says Benvolio with a smile. "It's a **masked ball**."

CHAPTER 2

A Party

Juliet is in her bedroom. She has a blue dress in one hand and a yellow dress in the other hand. She's looking at them.

The door opens and a woman comes in.

"Oh, Nanny!" says Juliet. "Please help me. Which dress is better for the masked ball?"

"Both dresses are nice," Juliet's nanny answers. "And you always look beautiful."

The door opens again. It's Lady Capulet, Juliet's mother.

"Tonight is a very important night," she tells her daughter. "You're going to meet Paris."

"Why is that important?" asks Juliet.

"He's going to be your husband!"

Juliet is **shocked**.

"I have to **marry** him?" she asks. "But I don't know him."

"He's a good man," says her mother, "and he has lots of money."

Lady Capulet leaves the room.

Juliet sits on her bed. She looks down. Her face is sad.

Her nanny sits with her and she takes Juliet's hand.

"Don't worry," she says with a smile. "It will be alright."

That evening, the party begins. There is music and food. People are wearing **masks** and expensive clothes. They are talking, laughing and dancing.

Juliet is with her nanny.

"Look, there is Paris!" the nanny says. "He's very **good-looking**!"

Juliet looks at him. "I don't like him," she says sadly.

Romeo arrives at the party. He's wearing a mask. His cousin Benvolio and his best friend Mercutio are with him.

Romeo looked at all the faces. "Rosaline isn't here," he says sadly.

"Stop talking about her!" Mercutio says. "Look! There are lots of other beautiful women here!"

Romeo looks but he doesn't like any of them.

Then he sees Juliet. She is wearing the yellow dress and she is smiling.

"She's the most beautiful woman in Verona… in the world! She's more beautiful than Rosaline," he thinks. "Who is she? I must speak to her."

Tybalt hears Romeo. He's standing with Old Capulet.

"That man is a Montague! Why is he here?" he says. Then he tells a **servant**, "Get my sword!"

Old Capulet puts a hand on his nephew's arm.

"Tybalt, don't get angry. This is my house – you mustn't fight here. Do you understand?"

Tybalt isn't happy but he doesn't say anything more. Then he leaves.

Romeo doesn't hear them. He only sees Juliet. After a minute, he goes and talks to her.

"Can I dance with you?" he asks.

Juliet looks into his eyes. "Yes, alright," she says and they begin to dance.

The music finishes and Romeo moves closer to her.

"Can I **kiss** you?" he asks.

She smiles. He's good-looking and he has very nice eyes.

"Yes," she says.

Romeo kisses her.

"Your mouth is warm," she says, "and you kiss very well."

They kiss again.

But then, Juliet's nanny shouts in her ear. "Your mother wants to talk to you!"

Juliet leaves. Romeo's eyes stay on her but he asks her nanny, "Who is her mother?"

"Lady Capulet," the nanny answers. "Juliet is her only child."

Romeo puts his hand on his mouth. He is shocked.

"She's a Capulet? Oh no! I love my **enemy**!"

The party finishes and Juliet goes to her bedroom.

"Nanny, who was that man?" she asks.

"His name is Romeo. He's the son of Old Montague."

Juliet sits down, her face very white.

"My only love comes from my only hate!" says Juliet. "What am I going to do?"

Romeo is in the Capulets' garden. He looks up and he sees a **balcony**. Juliet is standing on it, but she doesn't see him. She looks into the night, her face sad.

"Oh, Romeo, Romeo," she says. "Why are you a Montague?"

"I love you, Juliet," Romeo says.

Juliet is shocked. "Who is that?" she asks. She looks down. "Is it… Romeo Montague?"

"Yes," he answers, "but I will change my name. I hate it because it's your enemy."

"What are you doing here?" Juliet asks.

"I wanted to see you again."

"It's not safe," she says. "My family will **kill** you!"

"That's not important. I want to be with you. I love you!"

Juliet hears a noise from inside.

"Juliet! Where are you?"

"I'm coming!" Juliet says. Then, to Romeo, she says, "I have to go. Nanny is coming. Tell me quickly. Do you want to marry me?"

Romeo looks up at her. "Yes, of course I do!"

She sees love in his eyes.

"Tomorrow morning, find a **priest**," she tells him. "Send me a message with his address and I'll meet you there."

"Juliet!" her nanny shouts again.

"I'm coming!" Juliet answers. Then she looks at Romeo and she says, "Good night."

Romeo looks up at her. He smiles. "Good night, my love. Sleep well."

Juliet goes back inside. Romeo stays below the balcony for a minute or two. He looks up and he thinks about Juliet. He feels both happy and sad.

Then he walks slowly into the night.

CHAPTER 3

Husband and Wife

The next day, Romeo goes to see Lawrence, his priest, in a different part of the city.

"Juliet and I are in love with each other," he tells the older man. "We want to be husband and wife. Will you help us?"

The priest is **surprised**. "But you love Rosaline, don't you?"

"No, no," answers Romeo. "I loved her but I was wrong. Juliet is the woman for me."

"But your families are enemies," says the priest.

"I know!" Romeo says. "We must marry **in secret**... today."

"That's very fast!" says the priest.

He sits down and he thinks hard. "This **might** stop the hate between the Capulets and the Montagues. It might be good for both families... and for Verona."

Then he looks at Romeo and he says, "Alright, I'll help you. You can marry her here."

"Thank you!" says Romeo.

He starts walking to Juliet's house. But then he sees his cousin Benvolio and his friend Mercutio. He stops to speak to them.

"You look happy, Romeo!" says Mercutio. "We didn't see you after the party. Where did you go?"

"I had something important to do," he says.

"More important than your friends?" Mercutio asks with a smile.

Juliet's nanny sees Romeo from a window of the Capulet house and she comes out to speak to him.

Benvolio sees her. "Are you going to invite Romeo to dinner, old woman?"

"Oh, she wants to marry you, Romeo!" Mercutio says. They both laugh.

The nanny doesn't answer them.

"I need to talk to you," she says to Romeo.

"We're having lunch at your father's house," says Mercutio. "See you there." The young men leave.

"I don't like your friends," says the nanny.

"They're good men," says Romeo, "but they like to have fun."

"Listen," says the nanny, "Juliet is young. She doesn't understand men... but I do. Will you marry her or will you find a new love tomorrow?" Her eyes are angry.

"No, I'll never do that," says Romeo. "I love her. Look!" He shows her the priest's address. "We can marry today!"

"Oh, that's great!" says the nanny. "I'll tell

Juliet. She's waiting for information from you. She'll be really happy about this."

In her bedroom, Juliet waits. "Where is Nanny?" she thinks. "Love is fast... but she is very slow!"

A minute later, the nanny walks in.

"Oh, you're back!" says Juliet. "But you look sad. Is there a problem with Romeo? Tell me!"

"It's hot and I walked up to your room too quickly," answers the nanny. "I'm tired. I need to sit down."

"Nanny, please! What did Romeo say?"

"Oh, Juliet," says the nanny, and she puts her feet up on a chair. "Marry Paris, not Romeo. Your parents like Paris."

"Stop it, Nanny! I love Romeo and you know that! Please tell me! What did he say?"

The nanny smiles. She looks into Juliet's eyes and she says, very slowly, "He wants to marry you... today."

Juliet is really excited.

"Go to Lawrence the priest this afternoon," says the nanny. "You'll be Romeo's wife before dinner."

Juliet puts on her favourite dress and she runs to the priest's house. Twenty minutes later, she and Romeo are husband and wife.

Juliet is now a Montague. And the Capulets don't know it but Romeo is now part of their family.

CHAPTER 4

A Fight in the Street

It's a hot day. People often feel angry on hot days… and today, Tybalt is angry.

He finds Mercutio and Benvolio in the street and he goes to talk to them.

"I want to speak to Romeo," he says.

"He's not here," Mercutio answers. "You can't see that? Is there a problem with your eyes?"

"Don't start a fight," Benvolio says to his friend.

"Ah, here is Romeo," says Tybalt.

Romeo comes to see the group of men.

"Romeo, you're my enemy," Tybalt tells him, his face red and angry. "Take out your sword and fight me!"

But Romeo puts his hand on Tybalt's arm.

"Tybalt, I love you. I love all Capulets."

Tybalt doesn't understand. "What? What are you talking about?"

Romeo is now Juliet's husband but they married in secret. He can't tell Tybalt.

Mercutio looks at his friend, surprised. "You love all Capulets? Why did you say that?"

Romeo doesn't answer him.

Mercutio looks at Tybalt. "My friend won't fight you… but I will!"

He takes out his sword.

"No, Mercutio! Stop!" Romeo shouts. "The Prince doesn't want more fighting. He'll execute you."

But the two men don't listen. They start fighting.

Romeo puts his arm between the men. "Stop!" he shouts.

Tybalt's sword moves fast. It hits Mercutio under Romeo's arm. Mercutio **collapses** to the floor.

Tybalt leaves quickly. Romeo runs to Mercutio and Benvolio goes with him.

"Are you alright?" asks Benvolio.

"I need a doctor," Mercutio says.

Romeo takes his hand. "My friend…"

"I'm dying because your families hate each other," Mercutio says. "I hate the Capulets and the Montagues!"

A minute later, Mercutio dies.

Romeo starts to **cry**. Then he hears a noise. He looks up and he sees Tybalt. He's coming back.

Romeo stands up quickly.

"I don't want to see you!" he shouts. "You killed my best friend!"

"I'll kill you too," shouts Tybalt. "Then you can be together again!"

They fight. Romeo's sword is fast. He hits Tybalt. Tybalt collapses and, a second later, he dies.

Benvolio runs to Romeo. "Go, Romeo! Leave now! The Prince is coming and he'll execute you."

"Today, I married Juliet," Romeo thinks, "and, on the same day, I killed her cousin."

He runs to the priest's house.

Lady Capulet arrives on the street and she sees Tybalt's body.

The Prince is with her. "Who killed him?" he asks Benvolio.

"Romeo," Benvolio answers sadly. "But Tybalt started the fight. And he killed Mercutio."

Lady Capulet looks at the Prince. "Romeo killed Tybalt," she says. "Romeo must die."

Prince Escalus thinks for a minute. Then he says, "I won't execute Romeo. But he must leave

Verona and he must never come back."

Later, at his house, the priest tells Romeo, "You can never go back to Verona."

Romeo is shocked. "What? Oh no!"

"You're not happy?" the priest asks. "Why not? The Prince won't execute you. There are other cities, Romeo. The world is big."

"But Juliet is my world," says Romeo. "And she lives in Verona. I'll never see her again. I'll never kiss her again. Please kill me – I don't want to live!"

"Oh, stop this!" says the priest. "Listen to me."

"You can't help me," Romeo says and he starts crying.

"Are you a child?" says the priest. "Stop crying. You only see the bad things but there are lots of good things in your life. Tybalt wanted to kill you but you killed him. Prince Escalus didn't execute you. And Juliet loves you."

Romeo stops crying and he looks up at the

priest.

"Go to your Juliet," the priest says. "Visit her bedroom in secret but leave early tomorrow morning. Her family mustn't see you. Then go to the city of Mantua. That will be your new home."

"Mantua?" asks Romeo.

"Yes," says the priest. "Go to Mantua and wait. I'll speak to your family and Juliet's family too. They might stop fighting now because you two are married. And I'll speak to the Prince. One day, you might be able to come back to Verona."

Romeo listens to the priest's words and he feels much better.

"I'll be in Juliet's arms tonight," he thinks.

Then he leaves the house and he travels to the Capulet house.

CHAPTER 5

One Night Together

The night is ending and the next day is beginning. Together, the new husband and wife walk onto the balcony.

"Don't leave, Romeo," says Juliet. "It's not day. Look, there is no sun."

"In a minute or two, we'll see the sun," says her husband. "Listen – the birds are singing."

"I hate the birds," says Juliet. "Stop singing!" she shouts at them.

"I can't stay. I'll die."

"Yes, I know," Juliet answers sadly.

Romeo looks into her eyes. "I'm very sorry about Tybalt."

"He started the fight, not you," Juliet says and she kisses him.

Then Juliet's nanny runs onto the balcony.

"Your mother is coming!" she says. "Romeo must go. It's not safe for him here."

Romeo and Juliet kiss again. Then Romeo gets down from the balcony and he leaves.

Juliet goes back inside. She sits on her bed and she thinks, "Will I see him again?"

Her mother walks in.

"Good morning," she says.

She looks at her daughter's sad face. "You're sad about Tybalt, aren't you?"

She sits with her daughter. "Let's talk about something happier," she says with a smile. "Today is Monday. On Thursday, you will marry Paris!"

Juliet is married to Romeo but she can't tell her parents. She looks down at the floor and she starts to cry.

"Crying won't help your cousin," says Lady Capulet. "He's **dead**. Stop thinking about him. You're going to have a young, good-looking husband. You'll be very happy!"

"No, I won't!" shouts Juliet. "I hate him!"

Old Capulet hears the shouting and he comes to the room.

"Why is she shouting?" he asks.

"She doesn't want to marry Paris," his wife tells him.

"What?" Old Capulet says. He is angry and his face goes red.

"I don't love him," says Juliet. She's on the floor now, at her father's feet. "Father, please…"

"Stop talking!" Old Capulet shouts. His hand is near her face – he's ready to hit her.

"Please don't!" says the nanny.

Old Capulet puts his hand down again. Then he says, "Do you want to die in the streets? No? Then you will marry Paris on Thursday!"

He leaves the room.

"Mother, please help me!" says Juliet.

"Don't talk to me," her mother says, her eyes cold. "I won't help you." And she leaves too.

"Oh, Nanny," cries Juliet. "What can I do? I have a husband! I can't marry again!"

"Listen," says her nanny. "Romeo isn't here and you can't be with him. Marry Paris. He's better looking than Romeo and he's a good man. He'll be a good second husband."

She kisses Juliet's head and she leaves the room.

"Nanny speaks badly of Romeo and she won't help me," Juliet thinks. She feels angry. "I'll go to Lawrence the priest. He'll help me."

CHAPTER 6

Poison

Juliet arrives at Lawrence the priest's house.

"Can I speak to you?" she asks.

"Yes, Juliet. What is the problem? You look very sad."

"I have to marry Paris on Thursday!" she cries.

"Oh...," says the priest.

"There is no help for me, is there? Give me that knife – I want to kill **myself**!"

"Wait," he says, and he puts a hand on her arm. "I can help you."

She stops crying and she looks into his eyes. "How?"

"Go home and say to your parents, 'I will marry Paris,'" the priest tells her. "On Wednesday night, go to bed and drink this."

He shows her some red **poison**.

"Your body will feel cold and your face will go white," he says. "You won't be dead, but you will look dead. Do you understand?"

"Yes," Juliet answers. "But how will that

help?"

"You will sleep for forty-two hours," he says. "Then you'll wake up. Your family will think, 'Juliet is dead,' and they'll take your body to the Capulet **tomb**."

Juliet listens.

"I'll send a message to Romeo," says the priest. "He'll come to the tomb. You will wake up and Romeo will take you to Mantua. You'll live together there."

Juliet begins to cry again but because she's happy.

"I'll do it!" she says. "Thank you! Thank you!"

She kisses his hand.

The priest gives her the poison. Juliet goes home with it. The priest sends a servant with the message for Romeo in Mantua.

At the family home, Lady Capulet is talking to a servant. "Invite all these people for Thursday." She shows him some names.

Then Juliet comes in from outside.

"Where were you?" asks her mother. "You look happier than before."

"I went to see Lawrence, the priest," Juliet answers with a big smile. "I'm sorry about this morning, Mother. I will marry Paris."

"Ah, you're a good girl!" says Lady Capulet. "And you can marry him tomorrow! Why wait until Thursday? I'll tell your father."

"Yes, alright," says Juliet.

That evening, Juliet is in her bedroom with her nanny and mother.

"I'll wear this dress tomorrow," says Juliet. "But please leave me now. I'm tired."

"Good night," says her mother. She smiles. "Sleep well. Tomorrow is an important day."

The two women leave. Juliet gets into bed and she waits. After five minutes, she takes the poison.

"Tomorrow, I'll be with Tybalt in the tomb," she thinks. "Oh! My body feels really cold!"

A minute later, she collapses onto the bed.

The next morning, the Capulets all wake up early.

"Go and wake Juliet," Old Capulet says to Juliet's nanny. "We're ready... and Paris is here."

The nanny walks into Juliet's room and she goes to her bed.

"Beautiful Juliet," she says, "wake up. You're getting married today!"

Juliet doesn't move.

"Juliet? Juliet?" her nanny says. "Wake up, I said."

Then she sees Juliet's clothes. "Why are you wearing the same dress as yesterday?" she asks, surprised.

But, of course, Juliet doesn't answer.

She puts a hand on Juliet's face. "Why is your body cold?"

Then she starts shouting. "Juliet is dead! Lady Capulet! Come quickly! Your daughter is dead!"

Lady Capulet runs into the room and she sees her daughter on the bed.

Old Capulet comes in too. He sees Juliet.

"Our child! Our only child is dead!" They both cry.

"This is the saddest day of my life!" cries the nanny.

Paris comes in with Lawrence the priest.

"She's dead?" Paris says. He is shocked.

"Don't cry," the priest tells the family. "She had a good life. It's better to die young."

He looks at Old Capulet and he says, "Take her body to the family tomb."

CHAPTER 7

Together Again

Romeo wakes up in his house in Mantua. His first thought is of Juliet.

"I'll see her today!" he thinks with a smile.

The door opens and his servant, Balthasar, comes in.

"Do you have information from Verona?" Romeo asks. "How is my wife?"

Balthasar looks down.

"Her body is in the Capulet tomb," he says. "I saw her there and I came quickly to tell you. I'm really sorry."

"She's dead?" Romeo says. "Do you have a letter from the priest?"

"No," says the servant.

Romeo's face goes very white.

"Are you alright?" Balthasar asks.

Romeo starts to cry. Then he says, "Leave me."

The servant leaves. Romeo sits down and he thinks hard.

He remembers an old man in the next street.

He makes poisons.

"I'll buy some," Romeo thinks. "Then I'll go to the Capulet tomb tonight. I'll find Juliet and I'll drink the poison. We'll be together again."

In Verona, Lawrence the priest is waiting at his house for his servant, John.

John opens the door and he comes in.

"Hello," says the priest. "What did Romeo say? Do you have a letter from him?"

"No," answers the servant. "I couldn't go to Mantua."

"What?" says the priest, shocked. "Then who took my message to Romeo?"

"He hasn't got it," says the servant. "It's here." And he gives the letter back to the priest.

"Oh no!" says the priest. "That letter was very important!"

"I'm sorry," says John and he leaves.

The priest sits down.

"What can I do? In three hours, Juliet will

wake up."

Then he thinks, "I know! I'll go to the tomb and I'll bring Juliet back to my house. Then I'll write to Romeo again in Mantua."

But Romeo isn't in Mantua. He's inside the Capulet tomb and he's looking for his wife. He has the poison with him.

He finds Juliet's body.

"Oh, my wife, you're here!" he says. "This cold, black tomb feels warm because you're in it."

He takes her hand.

"I came here because I want to die with you. I want to stay with you always."

He kisses her.

Then he takes out the poison.

He drinks it.

"Oh, this poison is very fast!" he says. He kisses Juliet again.

"With a kiss, I die."

Romeo collapses. He is dead.

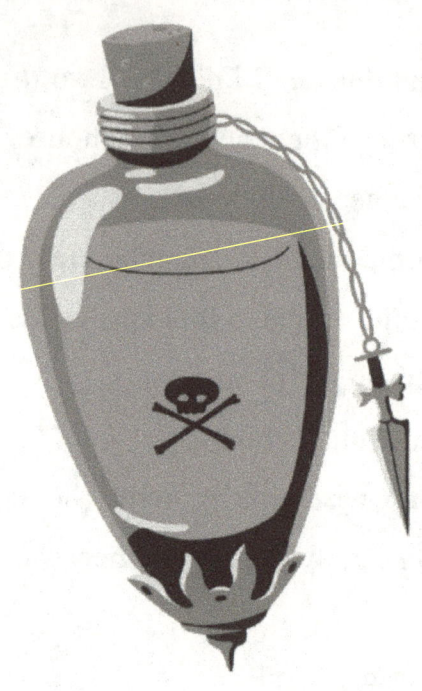

A second later, Juliet wakes up.

"Where is my Romeo?" she says. Then she sees him.

"Ah, Romeo!" she says with a smile. But, a second later, she sees a cup in his hand. "Oh no! Are you dead? Did you drink this poison?"

She looks inside the cup. "Is there any for me?"

There isn't any.

She thinks for a minute.

"I'll kiss you. There might be some poison on your mouth."

She kisses him. "Your mouth is cold," she says.

She waits but she doesn't die.

Then she hears a noise. "Who is that? I must be quick!"

She looks down and she sees Romeo's knife.

"Oh, Romeo, you have a knife."

She takes it in her hand.

"I'll kill myself with it."

The knife goes into her body and she collapses. A minute later, she is dead.

Later, the families find Romeo and Juliet together in the tomb. They are shocked.

The next day, Old Capulet and Old Montague meet on the streets of Verona. The hate between them killed their children and now, they cry together.

"This is a sad morning," they say. "Our children are dead and our hate must die too. From this day, our families will be friends. And we'll always remember Juliet and her Romeo."

THE END

Get free exercises for this book

Go to **ReadStories-LearnEnglish.com** and enter your email address.

You will get **exercises** for each of my books (vocabulary exercises, comprehension exercises and notes about British culture).

You will also get news about my new books.

MORE STORIES

A1+ Elementary

A2 Pre-intermediate

B1 Intermediate

B2 Upper intermediate

Words from the story

balcony (n)
a platform outside a window, with a fence around it

collapse (v)
fall down suddenly because you are hurt or very tired

cousin (n)
a child of your aunt or uncle

cry (v)
produce tears because you are sad or hurt

dead (adj)
no longer alive

each other (pro)
used when two or more people do something to one another

enemy (n)
a person who hates you and wants to hurt you

execute (v)
kill someone as a legal punishment

fight (v)
use weapons or hands to hurt someone (n, **fight**)

good-looking (adj)
attractive (comparative, **better looking**)

hate (v)
dislike someone or something very much
(n, **hate**)

in love (phr)
feeling a strong romantic emotion for someone

in secret (phr)
when you do something and other people don't know

kill (v)
make someone or something die

kiss (v)
touch someone with your lips (mouth) to show love or affection

marry (v)
become husband and wife in a legal or religious ceremony

mask (n)
something on your face to hide who you are
(**masked ball** – a party where people wear masks)

might (modal v)
used to say something is possible

myself (reflexive pro)
used to refer to the speaker as the object of a verb or preposition

poison (n)
a substance that can cause death or illness if you drink/eat it

priest (n)
a religious person who performs ceremonies

servant (n)
a person who works in someone's house and helps with jobs

shocked (adj)
very surprised and upset

shout (v)
say something loudly because you are angry, scared or excited

surprised (adj)
feeling shocked or amazed by something new or sudden

sword (n)
a long weapon with a sharp blade, used for fighting

tomb (n)
a room or place where a family keeps a dead body